Wolfgang Amadeus Mozart

Oiseaux, si tous les Ans

K.307/K.284d

A Score for Voice and Piano

British Library Cataloguing-in-Publication Data
A catalogue record for this book is available from
the British Library

ARIETTE
„OISEAUX, SI TOUS LES ANS"
für eine Singstimme mit Begleitung des Pianoforte
von
W. A. MOZART.
№ 307.
(Deutsche Uebersetzung von Daniel Jäger.)

Mozart's Werke.

CPSIA information can be obtained
at www.ICGtesting.com
Printed in the USA
LVRC02n0542060818
586092LV00006B/22